LESSONS FROM THE SECRET PLACE

INSPIRATION TO DRAW YOU CLOSER TO GOD

AUTOR
DA FÉ

EDITORA AUTOR DA FÉ
Rua Placídio Covalero, 341
Bragança Paulista | SP
autordafe.com
contato@autordafe.com.br

LESSONS FROM THE SECRET PLACE – INSPIRATION TO DRAW YOU CLOSER TO GOD

Category: Christian life

First edition – 2023

Author:
Raquel Tavares

Graphic and editorial design:
Author da Fé Editora

Editorial order:
Filipe Mouzinho | @filipemouzinho

ACKNOWLEGEMENTS

My heartfelt thanks to:

My loving Father: it is all because of You!

Scott Tompkins: your help was invaluable, may God reward you as only He can.

Heidi: your labor of love was a wonderful surprise, I am overjoyed you were part of this "delivery".

Delsine: I appreciate your willing heart and your help.

FOREWORD

My friend, Raquel Tavares is the right person to share this book with you.

She has spent untold hours in her secret place with the Lord. She and her husband, Beto, have listened to God and obeyed His guidance together since 1997 when they married. They have seen successes and failures. Raquel says, "When God tells me to do something, I don't need to understand it. I just need to obey, nothing else. The outcome is up to Him."

I first met Raquel when I taught in a writer's seminar at a Youth With A Mission (YWAM) center in Piratininga, Brazil, a ministry she and Beto founded. From there, they sent out hundreds of young missionaries to other nations. Many are still serving, leading, and shining for Jesus in different parts of the world.

During the event, attended by students from several areas of Brazil, Raquel's natural talents stood out to me.

Raquel was born and raised in Brazil, by parents who taught her to love God and the Church. Before meeting her husband, Raquel learned how to trust the Lord for guidance and for her material needs. She was still a teenager when she served with evangelist, Rev. Bernard Johnson in her home country. After training in a YWAM Discipleship Training School (DTS) in Los Angeles, she became a full-time missionary in a new YWAM ministry in São Paulo in 1994.

Following years of service in Brazil, Raquel and Beto obeyed the leading of the Lord to go to Italy. They expected to be missionaries for at least ten years there, but they returned to Brazil after only three. Their hopes and dreams had to be put aside for various reasons. Leaving Italy was one of the hardest things they had to do, but they knew was the right thing for them. Back in their home country, they got further training; Beto in coaching and leadership, and Raquel at university, studying literature.

In 2016, Raquel entered a harsh, lonely, personal desert. Her faith was tested to the limit. Everything was shaken – her beliefs, her view of God; her shortcomings and weaknesses were exposed. Prayer had always been a strong part of her life, but this was different. Her secret place became her only refuge and hope. She pressed hard into the Lord. In this place she learned the richest lessons. What she had known before, intellectually, became practical and emotional. While she was still in that lonely desert, she began to write this book. It has been published in Portuguese with two printings in Brazil.

Beto, Raquel, and their daughter Nicole moved to Portugal in 2020, again, at the leading of the Lord. As she prepared to launch the book in Portuguese in Brazil, Raquel felt led by

God to set aside part of the book sales money to help women at risk, a project called the Rubi Fund. It started with one of the women the Lord sent Raquel's way, a young mother of four who had recently found Jesus. This precious woman inspired Raquel to start the Fund. Raquel tried to help her, but tragically, this woman's former husband murdered her brutally in front of her children. This terrible event heightened Raquel's desire to help vulnerable women. Now with the English version, she hopes Rubi Fund, partially through sales of this book, will help save other women.

I know you're going to learn so much from Raquel. As you respond to the Lord, He will move you closer to Him.

Janice Cunningham Rogers
Author, founder of writing schools in YWAM, teacher and missionary in Kailua Kona, Hawaii, @janicecunninghamrogers

ENDORSEMENTS

You will be captivated by this divine love relationship between Raquel and Jesus. The sacred and beautiful lessons shared here will encourage your heart and increase your faith while you laugh, cry, and run to find your secret place with the Lord!

Linda Troyer
(Author of Rest Revealed - www.lindatroyer.com)

In Chapter 3, referring to the 2015 movie War Room, Raquel writes: "The secret place goes wherever we go and isn't limited to a geographic location." I met Raquel when she and Beto chose our international church in Cascais, Portugal, as their spiritual home. It became evident to me that we had welcomed a woman of spiritual character, integrity, and prayer. She writes from personal experience with authenticity and transparency. This is a book we all can learn from applying its precious teachings to our lives.

At the close of chapter 19 she admits, "I have several notebooks stored away that have decades of written prayers. I write what I don't want to risk forgetting ... as a testimony of God's grace and faithfulness to future generations." Welcome, Raquel to the world of authors. Keep on writing and publishing. You have a lot of insight, wisdom and wealth to share with the world.

Pastor Eddie J. Fernandes (D.MIN)
(Founding-pastor of Riverside International Church, Portugal)

This is a light devotional book, but do not take "light" as an adjective that dismisses its value. Quite the contrary, these heavy times that we live in require light readings that will elevate our hearts towards the Lord like helium gas. The stories Raquel shares with us are snippets of her spiritual journey of faith as a missionary in Brazil and Italy. Her circumstances might be unusual, but her struggles and victories are familiar to all of us, missions or not. Sometimes she is trusting the Lord's faithfulness for the provision of personal things that many people take for granted, like her honeymoon trip, for example; other times she is struggling to find inner peace; at other times, to balance giving of herself with staying whole. As Raquel climbs her own Everest of difficulties, she doesn't do it with her heart always full of faith, like we picture the heroes of Christianity. She cultivates a lightness of heart that is always faith-curious: "The Lord has been present before so maybe I will trust

Him again." Her stories point to God, not to herself, making clear that a successful Christian life is not about how strong we are but about how much we are willing to risk. I hope you enjoy the helium gas for the faith that this book provides.

Braulia Ribeiro
(Author and theologian)

Lessons from the Secret Place will take you into a deeper revelation of who God is and of His intense and personal love for you. Although this book is short and very simple to understand, in it Raquel has revealed some profound truths. I highly recommend that you use it as a daily devotional book for 20 days, meditating on one of the 20 principles contained in the book each day. By the end of this period, you will find yourself very comfortable abiding in that secret place with the Lord. Just as Raquel has shared with us in this book what she has learned in her secret place, you will not only have gained from this reading, but you will have many more lessons that God will teach you personally as you learned to abide in the secret place with Him.

Craig Hill
(Founder - Family Foundations International - https://craighill.org)

In Lessons from the Secret Place, Raquel takes you on a beautiful faith journey. In addition to being a beautiful book, the content it provides us with is incredibly deep. We learn about having a consistent life of prayer that will take us into a place of complete dependency and trust in the Lord. If you habitually set aside time to be with the Lord or struggle to do that, I advise you to buy this book. It is short and easy to understand but simultaneously profound, extraordinarily challenging, encouraging, and uplifting. In every chapter, Raquel asks reflection questions that will lead you to a path of spiritual growth. You will find yourself closer to God as you ponder and pray throughout the day. Your prayer life will be strengthened, knowing that Jesus is always by your side, no matter what. I highly recommend it!

Elba Dolan
(Theologian, specialist in Christian counselling, president of RDC (Regional Development Center) and pastor of Vineyard Belém in Brazil).

RUBY FUND

What is it and why it matters

I was already living in Portugal towards the end of 2021, when God caused my path to cross with a young mother of four. For the sake of privacy, I will call her Paula. She was a beautiful 34 years old woman, but looked tired and stressed. She was a new Christian, recently separated from her abusive husband, away from her home country, struggling to raise her children, in desperate need of help in every area.

The timing of our paths crossings was one of those things only God could have orchestrated. It happened a few weeks before I was to leave for Brazil to launch this book you are reading, original text in Portuguese. As I learned about her sad story on the day I met her, my heart was filled with a compassion that was beyond human.

After we said our good-byes, I walked into my bedroom, sat on my bed feeling overwhelmed. I wanted to do something practical to help her, so I wired her a small financial contribution in hopes to help her out with her basic house bills; I also connected her to the Benevolence Ministry of my church. However, I felt it was just a drop in her ocean of needs. 'She needs help in every area of her life, how I wish I could do more for her!', I thought. As the day went on, I could not shake that feeling and then, I heard a soft familiar voice, whisper: "Well, you are soon going to launch your book in several churches in Brazil, right? You can set aside part of the proceeds to help her and other women in similar situation." Immediately the name RUBI came to my mind. Ruby is a precious gem and I felt this is the message the Father Himself has for each precious woman in unfortunate circumstances: "you are so very precious to Me and you are not alone!"

Soon after, in Brazil, the book launch tour exceeded my expectations as I saw God bless the sales and the message He had put in my heart to share. I quickly sold the first one thousand copies and had another thousand printed. A small beginning, but I was thrilled to send the first few contributions right out of the Fund to bless Paula and a few other women.

I kept in touch with Paula, tried to encourage her in her faith and in her challenges. Also, the members of the Benevolence Ministry of my church showed pure love as they reached out to her and her children as much as they could. I was certain things would get better and Paula would eventually overcome this season of hardships. Never could I have anticipated what was to transpire only a few months after. On one fateful night, about a year after my first encounter with her, tragedy hit with the worst possible outcome: her estranged husband and the father to her three younger children broke into her home at night, brutally attacked her oldest daughter leaving her for dead, and stabbed Paula to death. Shocked with this tragedy, our precious family of faith pulled together in love, prayers and support at this dark hour as we said our last good-bye to our sister in Christ.

By God's miraculous hand, after a few weeks in a coma, her daughter survived the assault. She has undergone several head surgeries and is recovering slowly, but steadily. She is a ray of light and hope in the midst of such darkness. Soon she will start a new life in the care of her biological father. Members of Paula's family have custody of the other children and we pray they too will continue to heal from the tragedy and trauma of their mother's death.

I fully understand if your heart ached as you read this story. Our Father's heart aches unimaginably more. Life's complexities and all the pain in this world cannot always be understood, but I know this: our God can turn ashes into beauty! He touched my life through Paula and I am convinced it was His plan to make our paths cross for a greater cause. There are still many "Paulas" all around us in desperate need of our help and we can make a difference.

This is why I am so excited you are holding the English version of my book! I hope and pray for great results in sales and an abundance in resources to reach and bless as many women as possible through the RUBI FUND.

Know this: by purchasing a printed copy of this book you are blessing a woman in her time of most need! Will you please help spread the word about the book and the RUBI FUND?

If you wish to know more about RUBI FUND, to help and participate somehow, please reach out to me, I will be delighted to talk to you: raquel@viladolouvor.org or on Instagram: raqueltavares7244 or Facebook: Raquel Tavares.

Thank you and God's richest blessings to you!

Raquel

INTRODUCTION

On a morning in June of 2019, I woke up with this phrase in my head: *Lessons from the Secret Place.* I knew it was a title for a book and I immediately knew in my spirit it was God telling me to write. With it came ideas and chapter themes, so I set out to write. In a couple of weeks I had written 17 succinct chapters, knowing that it was a mere rough draft. The backbone of my draft was prayer and I illustrated through examples of experiences and lessons from my own journey with God.

I felt there was something deeper God had for me in this season that somehow included writing this book and though I did not grasp the whole of what it would entail, I responded to the Spirit's prompting and embarked on this new adventure with Him. In Mathew 6:6 Jesus gives instructions about our prayer life. He highlights the aspect of prayer being done to the Father, in private.

But when you pray, go into your room, close the door and pray to your Father, who is unseen.

Then your Father, who sees what is done in secret, will reward you. He was clearly confronting the behavior of the hypocrites in the synagogues, who would stand in public, praying out loud seeking to be praised by others. He instructed us to do the opposite.

I see 3 main aspects this command contains: 1) prayer must be a regular part of the life of a disciple; 2) it should be cultivated in secret; 3) it involves rewards from the Father. The point Jesus wanted to get across was that all of our life must primarily flow out of a private life centered in Him with the motivation to please Him first and foremost. The rewards should be the result of a life of true devotion, not the main goal to be pursued. We must cultivate our prayer life privately; however, the outcome of that intimate life most likely will overflow into a public sphere of some level.

Through the years, my prayer life has mostly taken place in my own bedroom; the bedrooms have changed, but I always find a cozy corner to serve that purpose, though the real secret place is an inner one. There, I have cried out for a deeper level of freedom and wholesomeness, I have asked and received spiritual and material blessings, or at times, I have just sat in silence when there were no words. I have been changed.

When I felt the Spirit's prompting to share some of my experiences, I trusted He had a reason for it. He is the Lord of my secret place and obedience was my only appropriate response. In doing so, little by little, I can begin to begin to catch a glimpse of the bigger picture as I go along. The beauty of obeying a commandment we receive from God is that we are completely free from the responsibility of the outcome. Though I know what I would like to see accomplished through this book, I feel the result is not up to me.

The illustrations you will encounter here cannot be reproduced for they are personal. However, the lessons therein can encourage you in your own walk with Christ. May this reading strengthen your faith and deepen your intimacy with Jesus. If that comes to pass, then I will have achieved what I set out to do with this piece of work.

Dearly,
Raquel

CONTENTS

CHAPTER 1

MY FIRST SECRET PLACE

Do not be anxious about anything, but in every situation, by prayer and petition, with thanksgiving, present your requests to God.
(Philippians 4:6)

Growing up in a family of eight children and in a city with one million people, it would have been easy to feel lost. Thankfully, I never felt that way. I think that's because prayer always has been part of our family life. As I child, I often saw my parents on their knees in their bedroom. Knowing they were praying for us kids marked us all for life. It also gave us a remarkable sense of security.

We lived in a small wooden house within walking distance of downtown Curitiba, bustling capital of Brazil's southern Paraná state. From a child's eyes, my street was perfect. It provided plenty of playmates and great places to play hopscotch, ride bikes, and kick a soccer ball.

At the center of our lives was our local church. When I was 10 years old, I joined its pre-teen choir called "Singing for Jesus." Our group had received a special invitation to sing at an orphanage in the Italian neighborhood of Santa Felicidade.

On that special Sunday, we would perform at the institution's anniversary celebration and stay for lunch afterwards. I was so excited, and I assumed my parents would be too. But on that long-awaited Sunday, Mom squelched my joyful anticipation.

"I'm sorry. No one is available to take you to the meet the choir." "Mom, I need to go! I can go by myself. I know how to get there!" "No, it's too far."

I argued with all my might, but it was of no use. I simply couldn't understand why she wouldn't let her little girl walk a few blocks by herself in this city that felt so familiar to me.

I burst into tears and ran outside. My stomach seethed with anger as I hopped up on the low concrete wall that surrounded our house. The part that divided the gate of our neighbor's home and mine was a square corner with just enough space to form a make-shift chair. I positioned myself there, crossed my gangly legs, and cried a flood of bitter tears. As I wiped them away, I felt a sensation of helplessness.

"Why does it have to be this way? I hate having to depend on the grown-ups," I moaned.

Suddenly, a thought occurred to me: My house is practically on the way to the orphanage where our group would be going! Filled with hope, I prayed a silent prayer: "Lord, please make the van pass in front of my house!"

I don't know how many minutes went by after that prayer, probably less than five. The only thing I remember is the sound of a horn. As I lifted my head to see, I almost couldn't believe it. The church van was stopping in front of my house!

The driver yelled, "Hurry, we are almost late!" The kids inside waved and smiled at me.

I didn't think twice. I jumped out of my concrete corner and ran to the van – so excited that I didn't look back and didn't remember to tell my Mom I was leaving. Having been raised in a Christian home, I had learned from my parents that Jesus answers prayer, and I had invited Him into my heart. But that day on the wall was my first watershed experience with prayer.

In the face of a seemingly insurmountable obstacle, my desire to go and honor Him was genuine. Even as a young girl, lacking in understanding of a lot of things, as I sat in solitude pouring my heart to God, praying seemed the most natural thing to do. When I experienced the answer to it just a few minutes later, I learned something: He wants us to express our desires to Him. Prayer is fundamental; the response is up to God. Looking back now, connecting a physical place to a spiritual posture, I realize that concrete corner was my very first secret place.

God was already aware of my transportation problem and other details in my life. I came to understand that what was important to me was also to Him. He was not so busy with the big problems of the world that He wouldn't hear the prayers of a little girl. When my prayer was answered, there was incomparable joy.

REFLECTIONS

The secret place is anywhere you can be alone with Jesus. The foundation is a life submitted to Him. The construction comes from cultivating a relationship in which prayer is a pillar. If He is already your Lord, how is your prayer life? It's in this place that our relationship with Him matures. Not one of our needs is too small for our Father of Love.

- **What was your first watershed experience with prayer?**
- **How did this contribute to your journey of faith?**

CHAPTER 2

PEOPLE LIKE US

But he said to me, "My grace is sufficient for you, for my power is made perfect in weakness." Therefore, I will boast all the more gladly about my weaknesses, so that Christ's power may rest on me.

(2 Corinthians 12:9)

I have always enjoyed reading. I remember sitting next to my mother at church when I was about five years old. I picked up the Bible on her lap, placed it on mine and began to leaf through the pages. Frustrated that I couldn't understand what was written, I begged my mother: "Please, teach me to read!"

Not long after that, my mother signed me up for the first grade at the elementary school near our home. At that time, children entered directly into Brazilian schools at age seven. I was six, but because of my mother's persistence, the school principal agreed to accept me a year in advance.

I was soon reading with a voraciousness that caused my spirits to soar. My older sister Cleusa also loved good books and, unbeknownst to her, I read almost everything in the book pile she kept next to her bed. It was mostly contemporary Christian classics such as: Run, Baby Run, The Cross and the Switchblade, The Hiding Place, God's Smuggler and Tortured for Christ, among others.

These books described heroes of the faith who endured unimaginable suffering and overcame immense obstacles. As a girl, I thought of those protagonists as extraordinary figures, who lived on a higher plane of faith and spirituality. As I matured, I realized they were normal people, not different from me and you. They all had limitations, fears, doubts, and insecurities. Biblical heroes of the faith were like that too. Abraham, Joseph, David, Paul, and Peter had character flaws and were subject to temptations like those we face today. All of them had reasons to doubt or to give up. How then did they have such faith and courage? Simply because they dared to believe in God's promises and to obey His will.

The Lord chooses to act in partnership with us. The Kingdom of God, that Jesus came to inaugurate, is demonstrated and expanded through us. We are also making history. Our stories may not be written in a book or shared with the masses, but they are part of the Lord's eternal story.

The heroes of the faith stories highlight their conquests. Remember, though, that they all were made of flesh and bone. Abraham was afraid and lied to free himself from danger (Gen. 20:2); David committed heinous crimes (2 Samuel 12:9); Jacob deceived his brother (Gen. 27:19); Peter acted cowardly and lied (Matt. 26:75). This should encourage us! Yes, they had weaknesses, but they became known because of their faith. Although the Bible doesn't hide their flaws, it reveals that they weren't defined by them. God called David, "a man after His own heart." These heroes never could have imagined their stories being a source of inspiration for centuries to come.

As I cultivated my own prayer life, I came to realize that the character of the heroes of the faith was forged in their own secret place. This place of prayer was one sure thing in their lives. And it must also be in ours. The secret place is not for perfect people, but for flawed ones, who desire more of God.

For we do not have a high priest who is unable to empathize with our weaknesses, but we have one who has been tempted in every way, just as we are—yet he did not sin. (Hebrews 4:15)

REFLECTIONS

We must not wait to be better people before making ourselves available for God's purposes. It is seeking God in the secret place that we can co-author a beautiful story with Him, even amidst opposition or in unfavorable circumstances. The secret place is for everyday people who don't allow their limitations to define them.

- **What weaknesses do you recognize in your own life?**
- **Have you brought them before God in your secret place? Even with those weaknesses, do you believe God will use you to expand His Kingdom?**

CHAPTER 3
PORTABILITY

And pray in the Spirit on all occasions with all kinds of prayers and requests. With this in mind, be alert and always keep on praying for all the Lord's people.
(Ephesians 6:18)

In the movie War Room, released in 2015, the protagonist, Elizabeth is a wife and mother with a family in crisis. Through the counsel of an elderly friend named Clara, Elizabeth begins to understand the reality of an invisible but very real "good versus evil" battle for her family. She then chooses to bring her struggles to the Lord and to ask that His will be accomplished in her home.

She creates a space for prayer in her bedroom closet and that corner becomes her "war room." There she pours out her heart with sincerity and her eyes begin to open and see the war taking place in the spirit realm. She seeks wisdom and strength to confront attacks which leads to a series of events allowing her to see God at work.

The "war room" she created was a symbol of the space she had given to God in her heart, the place in which He dwells. It would have been useless for her to have such a place if her heart was not fully surrendered to the Lord. The secret place goes wherever we go and isn't limited to a geographic location. Jesus frequently went to be alone with the Father, but at all times was completely submitted to Him.

After he had dismissed them, he went up on a mountainside by himself to pray. Later that night, he was there alone… (Mathew 14:23)

It is good to have a quiet place where we can seek God privately and with necessary solitude but that place, above all else, is a space within us. It has to do with a posture of our heart. It is a space where we joyfully cultivate a relationship that should be the top priority in our lives. It is a heart that recognizes its dependence on God; that knows daily fellowship is vital to nurturing this relationship. This kind of relationship is not about following a list of rules, but about cultivating a disciple's heart.

Before the birth of Jesus, the place of prayer and worship was the temple made by human hands. God's followers depended on the high priest to mediate their worship and the atonement of their sins. With the sacrifice of Christ, a new era was inaugurated. Now, the house God inhabits is within us. Today thousands of faithful followers and pilgrims still visit churches and sacred places as a demonstration of faith and devotion. As Christians, we are not limited to these places, for God speaks as we cultivate the secret place within.

Don't you know that you yourselves are God's temple and that God's Spirit dwells in your midst?
(1 Corinthians 3:16)

Many years ago, I spent a few months in Hawaii, USA, doing a training school with the international movement called Youth

With a Mission. The natural beauty of that place itself was an invitation. I found a nook atop a stone farm fence near the campus. Although I was tempted to trespass, I did not. But from where I sat, the view was spectacular. I climbed up on that fence almost every day to pray. It was an amazing time. I knew God was doing a deep work in my life, and that place is marked with the memories of that phase. This is one of the many nooks I've had throughout my journey for my alone times with God.

The nurturing of the secret place is a continual process. As you persist, it becomes more and more familiar and comfortable. It is the place you can be honest before God — totally you. With time, you will feel more at ease there than anywhere else.

Here are some practical suggestions that may help to cultivate your devotional moments:

- Choose a Bible version that you enjoy reading frequently.
- Have a notebook and pen nearby where you can write your prayers, impressions, feelings, responses, dreams and even draw if that helps you in your expression. This way you have a written history of your prayer life and it is a precious tool to return to time and time again to remember sometimes what we tend to forget.
- Besides the Bible, I like to read classic devotionals like: Streams in the Desert (Lettie Cowman), My Utmost for His Highest (Oswald Chambers), Mornings with Tozer (A.W. Tozer), Hinds' Feet on High Places (Hannah Hunard). Beyond devotionals, you can't go wrong reading the works of consecrated authors such as C.S. Lewis, Tim Keller, John Piper, N.T. Wright, Henri Nowen, Elisabeth Elliot, Lisa and John Bevere, among others.

REFLECTIONS

Although it is good to have a physical place where we can be alone with God, it is of utmost importance that we make space for Him in our hearts. We carry our secret place with us.

- **Has cultivating the secret place been a priority for you?**
- **If not, what steps can you take to nurturing your secret place?**

CHAPTER 4

LEARNING WITH HANNAH

Eli answered, "Go in peace, and may the God of Israel grant you what you have asked of him."

(1 Samuel 1:17)

I often have found myself thinking about Hannah of the Old Testament. Although married to a good husband, she was unable to bear children. To make matters worse, her husband Elkanah had another wife, Peninnah, who taunted Hannah because about her infertility. These provocations wounded her. Nowadays, being sterile is difficult but in Hannah's day it was also humiliating because procreation was considered the woman's principal function. I cannot imagine the frustration and sense of impotence she must have felt.

We do not know how long Hannah bore this burden, but it was enough time to bring her to the end of her strength. How many times had she poured out her tears before God? How often did she say, "Why should I pray again? I've already asked so many times and nothing has changed." What went through her mind on the day she decided to go to the temple to pray? We can deduce that she had prayed this prayer before. What had happened between the previous time she said this prayer and this one? We only know that she gathered the strength left in her, perhaps thinking this would be the last time. I know this feeling. A few times in my life I decided to give God one last chance to answer, as if I somehow had to persuade Him to hear and bless me!

God didn't need persuasion. He already had a plan for Hannah, and this was the time her destiny shifted. She poured out her heart before the Lord and He responded.

> *"The nature of divine goodness is not only to open doors for those that knock, but also in leading them to knock and ask".*
> (**St. Augustine**)

What do you and I have in common with Hannah? Simple: we all have faced obstacles and had longings that have caused us much angst. I have not faced the same difficulty as Hannah. When Beto and I prayed about having children, we asked the Lord to help us conceive quickly and without complications and so it was. Yet, we know many dear couples that have struggled with infertility. I can't imagine how that feels. However, I have had other painful longings. Who doesn't have unfulfilled yearnings and desires?

During Hannah's time, the temple was the place where God's presence was manifested, for the Holy Spirit had not yet been sent to dwell within us. The priest was His divine representative and had authority to bless the people. Thus, the temple was where Hannah wanted to be. She watered the temple court not only with tears, but also with her faith. When the priest saw Hannah's emotional outcry, he thought she was drunk! But upon recognizing what he was seeing as the longing of her soul, he comforted her: "May God grant your request," he said. And that's what happened! Hannah conceived and gave birth to Samuel, a boy with a special mission.

Hannah kept her promise to God: to bring her son to serve in the House of the Lord. Hannah's prayer shows us that the right place to pour out our longings is at the feet of the Lord, in the secret place. We also learn it is necessary to persevere, keep asking, for there isn't a formula to follow, but a relationship that encourages us to persevere in prayer, to continue to believe in "knock and it will be opened to you" that the Bible talks about. So then, grab onto this promise and continue asking. Who knows? Maybe it will be this prayer that will make your cup overflow and allow you to return home in peace.

REFLECTIONS

Think of an experience that brought you much angst. How did you deal with it?

- **Where did you seek comfort?**
- **What did you learn with the situation?**

CHAPTER 5
ABOVE FEAR

"If we take the generally accepted definition of bravery as a quality which knows no fear, I have never seen a brave man."
(George S. Patton)

Whenever I board an airplane, I know an unwelcome companion will show his ugly face. He appears when turbulence causes the airliner to shake, quake or lose altitude. My stomach becomes a knot, and it twists and tightens like an internal seatbelt. Cold sweats increase, shortness of breath sets in, and nausea sickens me. When my husband is seated next to me, I clasp his hand in my struggle to control my fear.

One time when he was seated a few rows ahead of me, I cried out, "Oh God! Please! Make the turbulence stop!" Beto heard me and shouted, "Love, calm down, it's going to be okay." Suddenly, an outstretched arm touched me. It was an elderly woman sitting one row ahead of me on the other side of the aisle; she was moved by my suffering. Quickly, I took her extended hand, and felt an empathetic squeeze. Perhaps she suffered from the same fear, though more discreetly. I will never know.

This is an example of a light kind of fear, one I have learned to live with because I decided I will not let it stop me from flying. But, what about fears that are deeper, that can leave me paralyzed, that sabotage me? I have those too.

The evil one purposes to wound our souls. Especially in childhood, evil causes fear to penetrate multiple layers of our psyche. Once infiltrated, it contaminates, steals, limits, diminishes, boycotts, cuts back, and dominates. We can't always give names to our fears because they are camouflaged behind some other emotion, such as anger or sadness. Their roots are so deep that we don't even know where to start. Once when I was going through a difficult situation, a friend said to me, "Face your fears, Raquel, or they will keep you hostage." It's true, but it is easier said than done.

I have learned it's useless to hide my fears, deny them or try to take shortcuts, for life always forces me to come face to face with them. If we don't voluntarily confront our fears, they will confront us at some point along the road of life. Job, from the Bible, suffered staggering loss, grief, and pain. To his friends he confided, *"What I feared has come upon me; what I dreaded has happened to me."* (Job 3:25)

Our fears leave traces that attract the enemy like flies to meat. One of his strategies is to observe our patterns and then he attempts to make our fears a reality. He wants to paralyze and destroy us. Like John and Stasi Eldredge said in the book they co-authored, Captivating: "The story of your life is the story of a long and brutal attack on your heart by the enemy who knows your potential and fears it."[1]

For everything that has happened in your life, especially those things caused by the enemy, God has a redemptive plan. Nothing is outside the realm of His redemptive power!

We have human reasons to fear, for the valley of the shadow of death is real. Even the great men and women of God faced it. David said, *"Even though I walk through the darkest valley, I will fear no evil, for you are with me; your rod and your staff, they comfort me."* (Psalm 23:4).

Most of the time fears won't disappear like a vapor, but we will learn to deal with them as the Holy Spirit teaches us and as we are perfected in His love. As God said to Joshua, *"Have I not commanded you? Be strong and courageous. Do not be afraid; do not be discouraged, for the Lord your God will be with you wherever you go."* (Joshua 1:9)

Recycling Fear

How do we fight fear? Yes, with courage. But that's not quite the right answer. The true antidote to fear is love! As 1 John 4:18 says, "There is no fear in love. But perfect love drives out fear because fear has to do with punishment. The one who fears is not made perfect in love."

What an incredible truth! Being perfected in love is a process. Our courage will come from a deep feeling of security that we can only find in the perfect love of God.

I recently asked God to show me more of the plans He has for my future. The answer came in a phrase that seemed somewhat vague: 'Joy and freedom are on the other side of fear.' I have had fears about my future, so I hid this word in my heart and continued to pray that He would lead me to this place of joy and freedom and

He did. Pandemic, war, and economic struggle have spread fear across the world, but I can live in freedom and joy because of Him.

He will empower us to face the tiger that intimidated us for so long, and we will then find it was just a little cat. This reminds me of a story about a great warrior king who conquered many cities.

When were prisoners taken, they were moved into a large room where there were archers on one side and a massive iron door with engraved skulls on the other. The king said, "You can choose to die by the arrow of my archers, or pass through that door. As far as I am concerned, that's where you will stay." Every prisoner would choose death by arrow.

After the war ended, a loyal soldier asked the king, "What is behind that intimidating door?" "Go see," he replied.

The soldier slowly opened the door. As he did, sunlight streaked through illuminating the room. Once fully open, he realized it was a path to freedom. The soldier now in awe could only stare back at his king. "I gave them all the choice, but they would prefer to die than to risk opening the door," the king said.

How many doors to joy and freedom have we not opened because we feared taking a risk?

REFLECTIONS

Think about the situations that cause you fear and how you have responded in the past. Even when fears are legitimate, is it worth it to be paralyzed by them?

- **In what areas do you see fear in your life and how has it hindered you?**
- **What steps can you take to move towards courage and love?**

CHAPTER 6
SUFFICIENT

"Comparison is the thief of joy."
(Theodore Roosevelt)

Who could say they have never struggled with comparison? When we compare ourselves to others, we typically conclude the other's position is better than ours. This confirms an already formed opinion.

Sadly, the things we admire in others are often superficial — good looks, wealth, fame, achievements. We may envy a certain celebrity but have no idea of the price they paid to get there. We attribute the success of an entrepreneur to luck, without knowing how hard they worked to achieve it. We see only stars when thinking of a popular singer, but never the tears that wet their pillow at night. We don't know the struggles behind all those perfect smiles on social media.

Comparison feeds off discontentment, ingratitude, and a lack of acceptance. It is rooted in a selfishness that ignores God.

One of Jesus' greatest miracles was multiplying the loaves and fishes. At the shore of Galilee, the crowd listened to His teachings for hours. Afterward, they were hungry. Amidst this great crowd was a boy who offered his lunch to the disciples. It was only enough to feed about two people, and in John 6:9, Andrew verbalizes what everyone else around was thinking: "Here is a boy with five small barley loaves and two small fish, but how far will they go among so many?"

The boy likely knew that others had more to offer than he did, but that didn't stop him from giving it. In the powerful hands of Jesus, it was more than enough! When I am tempted to compare my portion to other people's, the Holy Spirit reminds me that what matters most is to yield to Him what I do have, in obedience and faith.

When we entrust Him with what we have and what we are, He is responsible for the outcome. Here are steps we can take to help combat the comparison temptation:

Seek out your identity in God

Ask Him to show you how He sees you. Your Creator is very convincing. He spoke to me during a painful season of my life, and it produced long-term transformation.

At the time I was struggling with depression, grieving the loss of my beloved mother, and plunging into an identity crisis. Being married to a man whose gifting and talents are well defined, I found myself questioning my purpose, my gifts, my place in life. I felt that in my marriage, in motherhood and in ministry my life I was on auto-pilot. I thought that my gift wasn't defined when compared to my husband's. Like looking at an unfocused photograph,

I saw my self-image as blurry. I needed to know who I was in God's eyes!

He showed me at a worship event that Beto and I were attending. That gathering had many people who were sensitive to God's voice. One day, at the end of a teaching, there was an invitation for those who wanted to receive prayer. In that atmosphere of consecration I went forward, in expectation that one of them would pray for me.

Kneeling, with my head down and eyes closed, I quietly prayed, knowing at any moment someone would approach me. Although many times before I had seen God use Beto to give words of knowledge to specific persons, I assumed he surely would not be the one to approach me this time, after all, he was my husband and knew what I was going through. The question came to my mind: "God, certainly it is someone else that you will bring to pray for me, isn't it?"

Immediately after this thought, I felt Beto kneel down beside me and whisper in my ear, as if he had read my mind: "Love, I know I am your husband and the last person that you would expect a word from right now, but I need to tell you the vision the Lord gave me about you." What he described next struck my spirit like a bolt of lightning, bringing refreshment to my tired and confused soul.

"I saw you marching in a wide street of a big city," he said: "... out of the windows of the tall buildings along the streets, confetti were thrown and people were happily waving flags... you marched and danced and your faced beamed with joy as you looked up to the sky, arms swirling in the air. You were a mix of a cheerleader and a majorette, wearing an elegant uniform with vibrant colors. There was a large crowd following you and they were touched by the atmosphere: new converts, unbelievers, disciples. You were celebrating, bringing joy to them and to God."

I immediately identified with the vision. I was reminded of an occasion, almost a decade earlier, when I was living in the United States and had received a word that God would use me to bring joy to others. For many years this seemed like a distant dream. Now, again, joy was the center of this vision. I received this word with faith and let it feed my soul. I didn't worry anymore about having a defined gifting. I simply wanted to be who He had called me to be. No one has more power to affirm our identity than our Creator!

Celebrate your Singularity

You are unique! Most likely you have already heard that, but it is fundamental that this truth be assimilated in a most profound way — in our emotions and not just our intellect. You are beyond comparison, designed by a brilliant God, with a specific purpose. When God creates something, He does it with intention.

Dan Allender, an American Christian author, in his powerful book, The Healing Path, tells about a day when his son asked him: "Dad, am I here for a reason?" He responded: "Son, you are the only version of yourself that this world will ever know, and there is something about your life that will reveal something about God that no one else can."[2]

It makes me think of this verse from Ephesians 2: "For we are God's handiwork, created in Christ Jesus to do good works, which God prepared in advance for us to do."

Cultivate thankfulness and contentment

Make lists of the good things in your life, your relationships, blessings, the many reasons you have to be thankful to God. Keep a "Thankfulness Journal"; ask someone close to you to remind you to be thankful when you are complaining.

Rejoice with those who rejoice

When you are tempted to compare yourself with someone or to envy the success of someone else, seek out that person to congratulate them on their success and mean it. When we transform our comparison in a way of encouraging and edifying another, the enemy loses ground, and God is glorified.

Cultivate compassion

Open your eyes to the needs of those around you. When we are empathetic to the pain of others, we can deal with our own pain with more tolerance and acceptance. The temptation to compare ourselves loses its power when we see that our five loaves and two fishes are more than sufficient in God's hands.

REFLECTIONS

- In your secret place, ask God to search your heart concerning areas where you feel dissatisfied with your life.
- If you often compare yourself to others, what steps are you willing to take to have victory over comparison?
- Reflect on your five loaves and two fishes. Have you already offered them?

CHAPTER 7
SEEDS

Sow your seed in the morning, and at evening let your hands not be idle, for you do not know which will succeed, whether this or that, or whether both will do equally well.

(Ecclesiastes 11:6)

God plants in our hearts the dreams and plans He has for us. They need regular care to germinate and grow. It is our responsibility to seek out what those divinely planted dreams are and cultivate them.

This cultivating takes place in our secret place. Our prayers and praises nurture the budding plant until it finishes its cycle of growth and produces fruit. However, there are times when God tests our heart and asks us to let go of a dream. Our willingness to allow a dream to die, in submission to God, becomes fertilizer in the soil in which one day it can possibly be reborn.

For as long as I can remember, I have dreamed of travelling, learning new languages, and experiencing new cultures.

As a young girl, I studied English both at home and in school. I listened to English songs on the radio and on tape, I attempted to write down the words, singing together with the tracks to memorize them. My big dream was to learn English while living abroad, but for a Brazilian girl whose family had limited resources, this seemed unattainable.

One Sunday, a friend of my brother mentioned an international student exchange program called American Field Service. My mind went on high alert, and I began to learn more about it. A few months later, I heard that applications for the AFS program that year were being accepted. My brother, Isaiah, paid for the application fee to encourage me, a gesture of kindness that was so fitting to his big heart. It might only be a dream, I thought, but I need to take this first step.

Students approved for the AFS program get to spend eleven months in another country, living with a host family and attending public school for their senior year of high school. As I applied, I prayed, "Lord, I really want this, but I don't know if it is what you have planned for me. If it isn't, please show me. If it is, please confirm it and give me favor. I want your will for me."

The selection of candidates was done in three phases, it included a written test, group evaluations and an individual interview. Of the 180 applicants, 63 passed on to the second phase, and only ten to the third. I could hardly believe it when I found out that I was one of the ten!

Now, came the hardest part. The cost of the program was 3,600 dollars, which included airline tickets and expenses whilst being abroad. That seemed impossible as Brazil was deep in recession with compulsory deposits needed to be made by those travelling overseas. My family had no way of paying that price, and I feared that my biggest dream would be ripped away.

Then one of the volunteers at the AFS Club advised me to write a letter to the agency's headquarters in New York. In my letter I would explain my situation and make a counteroffer. In talking with my parents, we decided what we could afford (450 dollars) and proposed a payment plan. I then prayed over the letter and sent it. During the days that followed, I had to manage my roller coaster emotions and exercise self- control like never before. It was so hard to wait! When the answer finally arrived, I was stunned. My bold proposal had been accepted! I was completely convinced that the result was God's favor over me. The seed He planted in my heart now it was budding!

That year in the United States was a watershed experience was for me. My host family lived in Mount Vernon, a small town in Southwest Missouri, in beautiful Ozark Mountain country. They were lovely and made me feel welcome. Though not church-goers, they were very supportive when I connected to the local Assemblies of God Church and attended it during my stay. It was a time of so much growth. God's grace was shown to me in practical ways such as being able to speak fluently in English faster than I anticipated (perhaps also aided by the fact being quiet is difficult for me!) I met dozens of others exchange students from around the globe, got a chance to do some travelling in America and was able to see and do fun and interesting things. It broadened my horizons and enriched my life in many ways. Remembering it today, I think about how important it was for me cultivate that dream as a young girl. How it was good for me submit my heart to God and wait for him to confirm if that was His dream for me. Even with the obstacles which were very real, I learned that when God has a plan and we submit ourselves to His will, He promises to guide us in the process.

Miracles happen, and He receives the glory!

When we are submitted to God and ask Him to guide our steps, we must trust that He will. When a dream is born in our hearts and persists for a time, we can be sure that it is a dream God has given us. Dreams are seeds. It is the Lord that plants His will in us so our desires will be aligned with His.

"...For it is God who works in you to will and to act in order to fulfill his good purpose."
(Philippians 2:13)

How I love this verse! It says it is God who gives us an aspiration, a desire for something that He himself will fulfill. So then we pray, motivated by a sense of purpose and destiny. Then the most amazing partnership with Him takes place. All of us need to be seed recipients as well as sowers.

REFLECTIONS

We are responsible for cultivating the seeds that we recognize were planted by God in our hearts. We cannot skip stages. It is necessary to persevere in patience until the process is complete. If we place our hope in Him, we will rejoice in the results.

- **What seeds do you recognize that have been planted by God in your heart?**
- **How have you cultivated them?**

CHAPTER 8

THE WAIT

And so after waiting patiently, Abraham received what was promised.
(Hebrews 6:15)

Waiting is part of the secret place. In our click-and-go technical world, many people think it outdated and unnecessary, but it is an important formative process in humans just as it is in the natural world. The formation process of a butterfly is a good example. Their delicate movement and magnificent colors delight us.

However, to see them in their cocoon, it would be hard to believe that something beautiful would come of them.

First, a caterpillar emerges, a phase that lasts months. During this time, they produce strings that look like silk, that adhere them to the surface where they are. During the chrysalis phase a transformation process is taking place that will create a new and strikingly different insect. When finally ready, it will tear through the cocoon and emerge magnificent!

In the processes of our lives, the cocoon phase is not pleasant. We deal with uncertainty, discomfort, and fear.

Inside the cocoon is a solitary and dark place. We long for the freedom of flight. However, if we skip the necessary phases, we will jeopardize healthy development. It's in the phase when apparently nothing is happening, that the most profound changes occur, transforming a larva into a beautiful butterfly.

When we ask God for something, it doesn't just involve God answering us, but also implies that He will prepare us for receiving His answer. That is why, in the secret place, we are molded until the cycle is complete. May God help us to not give in and skip the necessary steps!

I learned this hard lesson while praying with my husband Beto for a house of our own.

After years of travel in our missionary work, we came to understand that God also wanted this for us. But years passed, and I began to feel discouraged because I couldn't see the possibility of this prayer being answered. Nonetheless, we continued to ask God to give us our 'miracle house'

In 2012, we purchased a small piece of land in Piratininga, interior of São Paulo state, but couldn't formulate a building plan. A few years later, dear friends with experience in construction made a proposal. Our land would be divided to build twin homes that would later be sold. After praying and sensing peace, we agreed to the partnership. They took care of everything, and when the first house was ready, it was put on the market for sale while the second house was being built. But a recession came, and the house that was for sale did not sell, so the construction on the second had to be interrupted. Up until that point we had not considered keeping one of the houses, simply because we didn't have the funds to pay the difference.

But one morning in early 2017, Beto said to me: "Love, why don't we speak with our partner about the possibility of buying the unfinished house?" There was a spark in his eye while he spoke and soon I was excited too.

After doing the calculations, our partner Bruno gave us joyful news that we wouldn't need to pay any difference. The unfinished house was worth exactly the same as our part in the partnership! We were thrilled to learn that, so in the months that followed, with God's grace we were able to raise the means to finish our house. Nearly a year later, we moved into it, immensely grateful.

Every day this house reminds us of God's generosity and how it is worth it to wait for his promises. It was a long wait, but this is the miracle home that we longed for, that I was convinced he wanted to give us. What incredible joy when that request was answered!

Because of this wait, my dependency on God grew, and I acquired more self- knowledge. During that whole time, some buried attitudes in my heart came to the surface that I needed to acknowledge and confess: impatience, ingratitude, and the tendency to complain. I understood that, for God, the transformation and maturity the wait produced in me were as important or even more than the realization of the request itself.

A detail to add is that throughout the years of prayer and waiting, Beto and I were always interested in the stories of those friends that had realized the same dream. We celebrated in hearing the details of how God had provided for them so they could have their homes. It was contagious and it nurtured our faith. It is impossible to anticipate or foresee when or how God will act, because undoubtedly, his ways are higher than ours, according to Isaiah 55:8.

REFLECTIONS

Waiting is not easy but becomes less difficult when we are deeply convinced that the process was initiated by God. Consider the areas of waiting in your life and what they have produced. Are they only a passing of time, or are they cultivating faith and hope in you?

Isaiah 40:31 says: *"But those who hope in the Lord will renew their strength. They will soar on wings like eagles; they will run and not grow weary, they will walk and not be faint."*

- **What are the things you are waiting for?**
- **How have you allowed the Lord to transform you as you wait?**

CHAPTER 9

CAUTION: PRAYING MOTHER!

Can a mother forget the baby at her breast and have no compassion on the child she has borne? Though she may forget, I will not forget you!

(Isaiah 49:15)

I am forever grateful for the gift of motherhood. When I refer to mothers, this includes biological moms and mothers of the heart. Every woman possesses this gift, whether they exercise it or not, and the secret place has everything to do with exercising this maternal gift. Motherhood is one of the most powerful ways we can learn about the loving heart of God.

A mother is moved by a visceral force and is absolutely powerful. Do you want to talk about female empowerment? Exercise your maternal gift and you will see how powerful you truly are!

I see this even in the animal kingdom. It doesn't matter if it is a chicken, a sheep, or a lioness, all females prioritize their young. The mothers make daily sacrifices for their offspring and if they young are threatened, moms would give their lives for them.

Women have a natural inclination towards spiritual things, a readiness for faith, and a sensitivity to matters of the heart that Jesus acknowledged. He honored the faith of a Syrophoenician woman (Mark 7:24-30) and a woman with a chronic blood issue (Luke 8:43-48). Their healings give us examples of the strength and sensitive spirit of women towards God. Jesus, in all possible ways, empowered women and elevated their condition.

My mother was a woman of faith too, and her love for Jesus touched me in numerous ways. I often found her kneeling to pray or meditating in her secret place (a quiet spot in her bedroom). I knew her prayer list included many things, but I believe her children were on the top of her list. Many times, I would kneel to pray with her.

Even when I was far away, I felt near, because her prayers maintained us close in spirit. As a child, I thought she had superpowers. Her prayers seem to rise to heaven much faster than mine. Today I know what her secret was — love. No one loves like a mother. While mothers are human and therefore imperfect, their love is the purest love on earth.

Of course, our love does not compare to divine love, but I am convinced it is still the closest we can get to it here on earth (Is. 49:15). That is why when we pray, a force comes from deep within that drives us. It is a compassion that takes hold of us and allows us to identify with the mother heart of God.

One experience I had with my mom often reminds me of the power of simple faith. I was preparing for a trip to the United States, and one week before my departure date I went out to buy some small gifts. Before leaving, I removed unneeded items from my wallet (including bank and ID cards), and I placed it in my cross-body purse. It was sunny day, and I had a delightful time shopping at with my friend Lu. But when I went to pay for some items, the zipper on my purse was open and the wallet was gone.

When I remembered that my travel documents were in the wallet, I froze. Without them, I couldn't go on my trip. And there would not be enough time to get them replaced. Lu and I went to the nearest police station to report my stolen wallet. But I left with little hope of recovering it.

When I returned home that evening, I collapsed onto the couch, exhausted. "What's happened to you?" Mom asked. I poured out the entire story, choked with tears.

"Well, did you pray about it?"

"Mom, I got so upset and confused, I didn't even remember to pray. Can you pray for me please?"

She sat down beside me and in a simple prayer, asked God that I would be able to find my wallet. Admittedly, I didn't have much faith it would happen.

The next day, I arrived at work discouraged about how much this loss would complicate my last week at work. My mind raced and my stomach fluttered each time I thought of how to get replacements for my documents. I took a deep breath, and as I did, the phone on my desk rang. I answered, and a man's voice spoke my name slowly, making sure it was me.

"I found your wallet," he said.

I was shocked, and it took me a couple of seconds to respond. We quickly set up a meeting place. After hanging up, I let out a sigh of relief. Immediately, I remembered my mother's prayer.

We met in a downtown bakery, and when he handed over the wallet, I saw that all my documents were there. "I found your wallet yesterday in a small bag on the street. There were documents from other people so you weren't the thief's only victim."

Before saying goodbye, I asked how he got my work phone. "I was looking for contact information, and the only number I found was on a small piece of paper." The number that led him to me was from a "chance" meeting with a business colleague as I was leaving work that previous Friday. We had talked about getting together sometime so I jotted down her number.

As I said goodbye to the kind man, it was impossible not to see God's caring hand in the succession of facts. No one can convince me it wasn't a perfect, God-crafted solution in answer to my mother's simple prayer of faith.

When a mother lioness sees her cubs being threatened, the world sees a glimpse of what fury truly means. Don't mess with a mother! When we perceive that the enemy is threatening our children, an extraordinary force moves us, and in the secret place, the lioness is awakened. She brings our needs to God in furious prayer, fused with faith and grit.

Behind a child who repents and is transformed is a praying mom. Behind a child who has been healed, is a faithful mother. Behind a child delivered from alcohol or drug addiction, is a mother who never gave up believing. Many a young person has been saved from life-threatening circumstances by such prayers. When no one else has hope, a mother holds on. Only eternity will reveal the true dimensions of a mother's sacrifices of love!

A mother's love is a responsible love. Because we have faced our own weakness while raising, loving, and molding another human being, we see how much we need help. This humbles us and makes us more dependent on God. Mothers recognize their mistakes and are more determined to make things right.

Motherhood is a universal symbol of warmth, protection, and love. It is in the secret place that these natural qualities are amplified by the strength of the Holy Spirit to wreak havoc on the kingdom of darkness. It is there that we find wisdom, strength, and everything else needed to be the mothers God has called us to be. We cannot do it without God's constant help.

In the recent movie, Breakthrough, a 14-year-old boy named John fell into a frozen lake and was underwater for fifteen minutes. At the hospital, his mother, Joyce, hears the worst news from the doctor. Before the lifeless body of her only son, Joyce begins to talk with God. In her angst and desperation, she pleads with the Lord to breathe life into her son. Seconds later, the machines start to signal a pulse and the whole team returns to witness the miracle. The boy stays for a few days in the hospital, in state of coma, while the whole town is moved to pray for his complete recovery – and it happens! God could not resist Joyce's cry. He resurrects her son and returns him to her completely recovered.

Mother, remember that your love is a motivation force with incredible power. For that reason, take your love to the secret place and bow before the One who knows your mother's heart. Pray as only you can and cry out as a mother with faith to move mountains!

REFLECTIONS

Think about how motherhood has affected your life, your role as a daughter/son or mother and what lessons have you taken from this?

- **How have you applied the force of maternal love?**
- **In what aspects do you believe there is still room to grow in this area?**

CHAPTER 10

GOING TO WAR

Put on the full armor of God, so that you can take your stand against the devil's schemes.

(Ephesians 6:11)

A battle is raging between the kingdom of darkness and the Kingdom of God. Those who embrace Jesus as Lord of their lives become targets of a ferocious enemy who hates God and his children. This enemy (Satan) has targeted you whether you realize it or not. You should be aware of this influence in our world, but not fearful. Our God is greater than our largely unseen enemy, and the Lord has assured us that the devil will flee when we resist him (James 4:7).

One strategy the enemy uses against us is to polarize opinions between believers about how he works. On this pendulum, some live in constant fear that they will be influenced by the acts of the devil. They blame him for things he had nothing to do with, particularly the consequences of their own bad choices. On the opposite side are those who minimize the reality of this war and almost never perceive when the enemy is at work. Neither extreme is healthy. We are called to live with the peace and confidence that God is with us, and He is our great protector. We are called to be aware of the enemy's intents and prepared to resist him.

As 1 John 3:8 says, The Son of God appeared for this purpose, to destroy the works of the devil. We have a role in this mission. Jesus calls us to be of sober mind, vigilant, conscious of the enemy for he is always prowling to attack (1 Peter 5:8). We should arm ourselves spiritually, without fear and without giving Satan the focus that belongs to Christ. Much of this preparation happens in the secret place, for it is where spiritual battles are waged and won. I love this verse because it shows the great power of waging war in the Spirit:

For though we live in the world, we do not wage war as the world does. The weapons we fight with are not the weapons of the world. On the contrary, they have divine power to demolish strongholds.

(2 Cor 10:3-4)

We cannot place responsibility on the enemy for all our struggles. Many times, the battle is against our own flesh, against our own human passions. Whatever the origin, we can be sure of one thing — the devil wants us to fall and fail. We cannot deceive ourselves. He wants us dead or at least neutralized.

A few years ago, I discerned a clear attack of the enemy against my daughter: he used an old strategy of his to attack her identity. An evil scheme we are all vulnerable to, but teenagers even more so, as they are in period of establishing who they are and their self-worth. Immediately, I went to war in my secret place to fight first in the spiritual realm and to seek heavenly strategies. In this case, I was doubly motivated, as Christ's disciple but also as a mother. By nature, mothers are nurturers, but hell saw this mother's fury when it targeted my girl!

I had never felt such motivation to fight! When I realized the danger lurking around my daughter, I was taken by a holy wrath, an indignation, a fury against evil, a desire to show the devil that he would have to come through me and an army of heavenly angels before he could touch her!

Spiritually speaking, I felt like a lioness. It was an incredibly enriching experience! The following quote is attributed to several people, and I found it to be exactly what I experienced: "You don't know your own strength until being strong is your only option." I would only add that we can only be strong in the strength of the Lord.

When we are tempted, attacked, or encountering ob stacles, it is in the secret place that we will be strengthened. We stand on the solid ground of His Word and allow God to guide us to victory in this invisible war.

The LORD is my strength and my shield; My heart trusts in Him, and I am helped; Therefore, my heart exults, and with my song I shall thank Him (Psalm 28:7).

REFLECTIONS

God has dreams, plans, and purposes for each of us. Opposition will come. However, our focus should be on God and what He is doing, for we know that we have already won.

- **What is your perspective on spiritual warfare? Have you been unaware of the devil's activity in your life or taken your focus off God? Think about a memorable experience in which you sensed spiritual resistance. What did you learn from it?**

CHAPTER 11
DESERTS

"Therefore, I am now going to allure her; I will lead her into the wilderness and speak tenderly to her."
(Hosea 2:14)

It is impossible to go through life without passing through a few deserts — uncomfortable places and times in which we are confronted and tested. We don't go there voluntarily. The desert often slams us like a dust storm in the form of family crisis, a serious illness, an accident, death of a loved one, natural or financial disaster, or a crippling disappointment. If you have been through a desert, you know what I mean.

Jesus was especially close to His Father in the desert times, and we can be too. The secret place becomes our refuge, and it is where deep transformation happens.

Think of the desert like this:

A place of solitude

It is only you and God. There are situations in which no one else, regardless of how well intentioned they may be, can help you or truly understand what you are experiencing. In the desert, the attitude of your heart is tested. Solitude is not intended to push you away from God. On the contrary, it brings you closer because He has your full attention.

A place of purification

Here our beliefs, convictions, faith and values are tested and refined. The superfluous is banished and only the essential remains. It is only in the silence of the desert that we can hear what the rumor and loudness of everyday life drowns out. It is the preparation for a new phase or transition to something important. It is the test before the promotion.

In 1 Chronicles 12, David went through a time in the desert before becoming king. Joseph had his time in the desert before attaining the influence foretold in his dreams. John the Baptist and Jesus also experienced the desert before beginning their ministries (Luke 4:1).

When I am in a desert season, I struggle, I question, I try to understand and too often, I look for a shortcut but find that God is not in a rush to get me out. Romans 8:28 says, "And we know that in all things God works for the good of those who love him, who have been called according to his purpose." But while in the desert, I usually cannot see how that situation will "work together for my good."

In my secret place I come face-to-face with my weakness and at times, I can't even muster words; I spill my tears in silence. Only when I surrender to His will do I get a glimpse of the richness of the desert place.

I like how 1 Peter 1:7 describes these times: These have come so that the proven genuineness of your faith—of greater worth than gold, which perishes even though refined by fire—may result in praise, glory and honor when Jesus Christ is revealed.

A place of miracles

The circumstances of the desert open opportunity for the miracles and manifestation of God's power. With our focus solely on Him, surrendered, we pray for our needs, and we see them miraculously fulfilled. Just as He supernaturally provided for the Hebrew people, He will care for you and me in our deserts. He reminded Israel: Your clothes did not wear out and your feet did not swell during these forty years. (Deuteronomy 8:4).

We certainly would prefer that our life lessons weren't so difficult, but no other place can teach us like the desert. While writing this book, I am experiencing a desert season, and I don't know when it will be over. I do know that the Father is leading me through it, and I will come out on the other side safe. I have learned about brokenness and dependency on God like never before. With Him by my side, I know this season won't destroy me but will make me more like Jesus.

I know this seems like a buzzword, but one thing has been fundamental in this phase is the exercise of living one day at a time. This approach is so hard for someone like me because I love to plan and dream about the future! My daily prayer has been: "Father, what do you have for me today?" Jesus knew how much we would need this direction when He said: "Therefore do not worry about tomorrow, for tomorrow will worry about itself. Each day has enough trouble of its own" Matthew 6:34.

A place of intimacy

Embrace the Lord in your desert place. His voice, beauty and gentle touch feel much nearer there. You will find Him in subtlety and sweetness, in power and strength, and in captivating revelations. In the blazing sun as your shade. On cold nights, He will warms us. As our love for Him grows, we will find Him in all our circumstances of life.

Before the desert, our experiences with God are often hearsay. But afterward, we experience new intimacy that was born in the secret place. We are not the same and it is impossible to hide it. My ears had heard of you but now my eyes have seen you. (Job 42:5)

REFLECTIONS

Whenever we find ourselves in the desert, it is difficult initially to find reasons for being thankful, nonetheless, persevering will result in precious fruit. From the dryness, scarceness, discomfort and pain, something new and beautiful is forged.

- **What have been your most memorable desert moments?**
- **What transformations took place as a result?**

CHAPTER 12

SILENCE

In relationships, silence is for mature friendships.
(Raquel Tavares)

Take a moment to dive into your memories. Think about someone with whom you have a deep friendship. Now remember your first conversations with that person. I'm sure you asked and were asked many questions in getting to know one another. You spoke of things you like, your family, your work and, as you grew closer, shared your joys, disappointments, and dreams. In a long and close relationship there are hundreds of such dialogues, but as friendship and familiarity grow, so does a new kind of intimacy.

Words become less necessary. Often all you have to do is look at your friend, and you know exactly what they are thinking or feeling. In these mature friendships, there is no fear of silence. When you know and trust, you don't need long explanations.

But in my relationship with God, I find silence frustrating. I want to make sense of things and know the "whys." Many times, I have encountered the silence of God in my secret place. Anguished, I pray, I weep, I cry out, but the gates of heaven seem insurmountable. I quiet myself to hear even a whisper, but nothing. I have zero control. God doesn't speak or act when or how I want. He expects me to wait and listen.

Silence bothers us and leaves us at the mercy of our own conclusions. Silence imposes uncertainty on us, and for this very reason it is the ground that fertilizes faith, stimulates hope, and purifies motivations.

"Raquel, there is a cyst in your left breast." The doctor's explanation of my ultra- sound results, hit me like lightning one morning. My mouth went dry, and my stomach churned. She said she would schedule a biopsy as soon as possible, but my mind was racing to other things. Two of my sisters had breast cancer. In that moment, what began as a routine check-up, suddenly became a crossroads.

Eighteen agonizing days passed before I got the results. The wait was tense, full of hope, full of fear, and too many feelings to list here. "I will take it one day at a time. I won't suffer before it's time," my mind said in one moment. Then in the next, "It's better for you to prepare for an undesirable result and have a plan B". On the same day, I would imagine myself without hair and that frightened me. All of this happened in the silence, in the absence of certainty, in the agony of suspense and amidst my daily tasks as a mom, housewife and co-worker.

When uncertainty knocks on our door and the fragility of life faces us head-on, the silence from the outside contrasts with the noise from the inside. I had never been afraid of having breast cancer, but that time, the silence forced me to deal with some ghosts, to rethink some things and consider reactions in the case of worst coming to pass. Those eighteen days passed at snail's pace. In the end, the two-ton weight was lifted when the results showed that it was only a benign cyst. I sighed a breath of relief and life returned with its normal noise.

Silence still visits my secret place every now and again. Over time, I have come to learn that the silence of God can signal a few of the following situations. This is not an exhaustive study, only some of my observations:

- I am not asking well if I am requesting something that doesn't align with the Word of God, that will be edifying for me or bring Him glory. When you ask, you do not receive, because you ask with wrong motives, that you may spend what you get on your pleasures. (James 4:3)
- I am not ready for what I am asking or to hear a negative response.
- We simply live in a fallen world and God's Kingdom has still not been manifest in its plentitude. There are many questions for which I don't receive answers,

> even when seeking in prayer. In our humanity we are subject to sickness, doubt, angst, and pain that are not always due to lack of faith or sin. I have told you these things, so that in me you may have peace. In this world you will have trouble. But take heart! I have overcome the world. (John 16:33)

Beyond these possibilities, there is still another that brings me much comfort: I have learned to interpret the silence of God as a sign of our solid friendship, of my trust in His character and His trust in my spiritual maturity. Even when circumstances shout the opposite, God's silence would never imply indifference or omission on His part. I now accept with thankfulness that which He chooses to reveal, and I trust that what I don't see or understand is covered under the mystery of His sovereignty and love.

For now we see only a reflection as in a mirror; then we shall see face to face. Now I know in part; then I shall know fully, even as I am fully known. (1 Corinthians 13:12)

When God is silent, we ask Him to search our hearts for hidden sin, but if we perceive a clean conscience, we can rest peacefully. A solid friendship allows for silence. A mature relationship with Christ means: I trust that He alone knows what is truly best for me. I apply the Scripture: *"But I have calmed and quieted myself, I am like a weaned child with its mother; like a weaned child I am content."* (Psalms 131:2)

REFLECTIONS

Silence is part of the secret place. Sometimes it is God's silence. Other times, it is ours. In times such as these, mutual trust is sufficient.

- **Have you ever or are you presently experiencing God's silence?**
- **How has it affected you? What has it produced in you?**

CHAPTER 13
EXPECTATIONS

"The better part of our lives is spent waiting what is to come."
William Hazlitt

Expectations. Oh, what weight that word can carry and what contradicting emotions it can produce! Life without expectations produces boredom while life with unrealistic expectations guarantees disappointment. I have concluded that balancing expectations is one of the most difficult things in life.

Expectations are a part of our secret place. When we pray for something or someone, we involve our emotions, our time, our very soul. Prayers soaked in tears generate hope and expectation of a response. No matter how close I am to God, my humanity can still create expectations.

So, where do they come from? Why is it so easy to create them and feed them? The human soul has been designed to dream, desire and long for. To have expectations is to risk. They are birthed from promises, from the dreams and plans of every beating heart. They can be big or small, good or bad, reasonable or not.

When I receive a promise or a word from the Lord about something specific, I expect it will come to fruition. Sarah and Abraham received the promise of a son (Genesis 15 and Romans 9:9) and they waited expectantly until it was fulfilled. It would have been humanly impossible for them not to cultivate expectations or imagine how it all would happen.

Pessimists say it is better to not have expectations so then, whatever comes, is gain. Visionaries say life without expectations is not a real life. I admit that expectations have caused much suffering and disappointment in my life. Ironically, though, some of the best things to ever happen to me were not planned and came as wonderful surprises. While we must be careful not to let expectations rule us, it's not good to uproot them all together. There is pleasure in expectation that something good is about to happen. One of the most famous quotes in world literature is found in the delightful The Little Prince, by Antoine de Saint-Exupèry. It describes the pleasure in anticipating being with a loved one: "If you come, for example, at four in the afternoon, at three o'clock I will begin to feel happy."[3]

The Challenge

In relationships, if I don't seek to know the other person's expectations or if I don't communicate my own, my mind tends to deduce things that aren't necessarily true. In my relationship with God, I have felt hurt many times when I have created expectations of how He would accomplish something. Relief comes in knowing that He intimately knows me and doesn't have unrealistic expectations about me.

The challenge is to manage my own imagination while I wait, try to resist the temptation to anticipate and to make my own mental molds fit the when and how of the things I pray for. We experience confusion, doubt, and disappointment as part of our journey, but God doesn't get disappointed with us for it. He continues faithfully dedicated to loving us with a fierce and immovable love. I have learned that God is commitment to His word and His promises, not to my expectations. Rest comes when I submit my expectations to the Lord and trust that His love and eternal perspective will produce the best result.

REFLECTIONS

As you ponder on your own experiences with expectations, consider the following questions:

- **What place do expectations have in your secret place?**
- **Contemplate and comment on your reaction when your expectations have been frustrated.**
- **How would you like to manage expectations from now on?**

CHAPTER 14

THE BASEMENT

So do not fear, for I am with you; do not be dismayed, for I am your God. I will strengthen you and help you; I will uphold you with my righteous right hand.

(Isaiah 41:10)

Eyes closed, I envision myself in a spacious and beautiful house, with large windows where sunlight pours in and fresh breezes ruffle the curtains. It is the kind of home I want to live in. But in order to fully enjoy living in a place of light and freedom I need to visit another part of the house. Beyond the main entrance, a small door leads to a stairway and a basement. Basements are often dark and stuffy. I truly dislike places like this. They smell of dust and mold and bring back memories most of us would like to keep buried.

Our soul also has a door that leads to a basement. Some people never realize this. Others know of it, but never venture there. That dark place hides secrets, wounds, and traumas. To live in peace and joy in our envisioned house, we all must brave the basement at some point.

It is not something we can or must do on our own. The Lord stands at the door to those stairs. With extended hands and love-filled eyes, He invites you to descend. Initially, the idea is terrifying and everything in you says, "Run!" But what alternative do you have? The pain festering in the basement is still there, despite all you have done to get rid of it. Jesus gently says, "Let me go with you. I will give you the courage to overcome."

Our hesitancy is understandable. Who wants to come face-to-face with suffering and loss? Who wants to revisit the cruelty of abuse, the trauma that stole your sense of worth and dignity? Many of us fill our lives with enough work and distractions that we rarely think of the basement. Life rolls on, and we persuade ourselves that it will all be okay. But some nights when you lay your head down on your pillow, a voice you can't silence whispers that it's not. Something needs to be confronted, healed, and filled — and time doesn't do that. The more years that pass, the louder that voice becomes. We can continue to ignore it or... descend the stairs to the basement.

Why are we afraid?

We fear the basement because we don't have control over it and because we believe we cannot bear the pain revisiting it will cause. We don't know what else we could find underneath the boxes or how long it will take to clean up the mess. Some secrets are so well hidden and so painful that even with Jesus' help we don't feel able to expose, verbalize, confess, and forgive them. To do so will change us, and we don't feel ready. We try to convince ourselves that to stay on the floor above where we have more control is safer. Is it really?

The extended hand beside the door to the basement is an invitation, not a requirement. Only you can know when you are ready to put your hand in His. What gives you strength to do it is the same that gave me strength when I saw Him there: He goes ahead of me, He is the guide. He knows the basement better than anyone and knows how to move around in the dingy and dirtiness. The Guide knows the right boxes to open and when to do it.

If I had to do it myself, I wouldn't. I couldn't handle it. But that irresistibly compassionate look in His eyes speaks without words, giving me courage to step forward: "I have waited for you here for a long time, but only now are you ready. Don't be afraid, I know this basement well and we are going to do this together. I won't leave you alone for a second. This will free you and heal you. When we are done, you won't be the same. When you return to the floor above, it will be a place of peace and rest instead of an escape."

To go down to the basement and come face to face with reality, is the starting place for the mysterious healing workings of God. He doesn't work in denial or in escape. In fact, the basement is part of the house. Just because it is hidden doesn't mean it doesn't exist or doesn't have influence over us. Only that which is recognized and confronted can be resolved and healed. He knows how much our wounds affect us. For this reason, He has compassion on us and desires to heal our pain and afflictions.

For the word of God is alive and active. Sharper than any double-edged sword, it penetrates even to dividing soul and spirit, joints and marrow; it judges the thoughts and attitudes of the heart.

(Hebrews 4:12)

REFLECTIONS

The secret place will challenge us to descend to our own "basements." Presently, I find myself in my own and although challenging, I am not afraid, for my Guide is with me. I know this will result in freedom and healing.

- **Are you aware of the basement of your soul?**
- **Have you ever received an invitation to descend?**
- **What has kept you form descending?**

CHAPTER 15

THE "C" FACTOR

Do not be anxious about anything, but in every situation, by prayer and petition, with thanksgiving, present your requests to God.

(Philippians 4:6)

"C" is for control. Until recently, if someone had told me I was acting in a controlling manner, I would have been surprised or even offended. I had never thought of myself that way. But recently, God exposed this attitude as He zoomed in on one aspect of my life.

It related to my relationship with my then teenage daughter. Being the mother of an only and strong-willed child, I had been trying hard to "help" her achieve her goals. Nothing wrong with that – except the way I was handling it. I was telling her what I thought were the necessary steps she "must" take and when. Obviously, I created expectations, which were frustrated when things did not go with the speed or intensity I thought they should.

The Lord showed me I was pressing too hard in my own strength. I thought I would manage this situation. But we can never truly be in control when it involves someone else, can we? I needed to surrender my controlling attitude to Him.

"We should not do for others what they can do for themselves". These words of wisdom are common knowledge, but oh how difficult it still is for me as a mother to put this into practice!

Why do we hold on to control? Because we don't trust. Why don't we trust? We want to avoid pain, suffering, being betrayed, or losing something. Our goal in relationships should be for the Lord to the transforming work, instead of viewing others as if they were projects. It is simple if we ask ourselves, "How do I feel when someone treats me that way?" Not good. The "project" approach in relating communicates that in order to be accepted, one must change; and the truth is, no one likes being forced to change.

Only after we have wasted precious time and energy attempting to control others or have hurt people we love, do we come to realization we can't change others. We can only change ourselves and that is hard enough.

In our roles of parents, leaders, and in other business or social functions, we continually make decisions that affect others. We must do so without using excessive control. How can I know when I have gone too far? By asking yourself whether what you are doing is legitimate care or thinly disguised manipulation.

Surrendering to rest

Like a traveler carrying a backpack, I had gotten used to carrying so many weighty things in mine. But the extra weight was not what God had intended for me. I was confusing being controlling with being strong. No wonder I was so exhausted! Yes, surrendering control feels scary at first. In the secret place, God showed me I needed to let go of the excess load. I learned that, when I do more than I need to or that I should, I pay a price, and the cost is always too high.

The invitation Jesus gives in Matthew 11:28-30 has been essential to my learning to yield to the One who truly is in control and can change people and situations:

> Come to me, all you who are weary and burdened, and I will give you rest. Take my yoke upon you and learn from me, for I am gentle and humble in heart, and you will find rest for your souls. For my yoke is easy and my burden is light.

The key to renouncing control is trust. "Do you trust me?" It is a simple but provocative question Jesus keeps asking us. It is impossible to control and trust at the same time. It is either one or the other. God challenges us to trust that His yoke is easy and light, and it is the only one that won't break us.

Who wouldn't want a light burden? It's intriguing that we grow accustomed to carrying heavy burdens due to our stubbornness. Deep down, we subtly and deceivingly believe we can do a better job than God. In the end, though, only those who trust are capable of surrender.

Control is exhausting, presumptuous and reveals an unbelieving heart. I was quite shocked to see such attitudes in my own heart. It is truly freeing when we decide to empty the space that control occupies. Then our soul receives the relief and rest it needs!

When anxiety was great within me, your consolation brought me joy.
(Psalm 94:19)

Don't be discouraged if anxieties reoccur. Frequently in the secret place, I surrender mine and leave lighthearted only to have them pop back the next day or be beset by new worries! By God's grace, we can choose to surrender our will to Him daily. As we grow closer to His heart, a beautiful thing happens – that "C" will then be for confidence that comes straight from heaven!

Let us acknowledge the LORD; let us press on to acknowledge him. As surely as the sun rises, he will appear; he will come to us like the winter rains, like the spring rains that water the earth."
(Hosea 6:3)

REFLECTIONS

Contemplate how you deal with control, especially in regards to your relationships.

- **How do you evaluate yourself in this regard?**
- **Since control is often a blind spot, has someone ever said you need more balance in this area? If so, what steps have you taken or intend to take?**

CHAPTER 16

WRESTLING WITH GOD

Then the man said, "Your name will no longer be Jacob, but Israel, because you have struggled with God and with humans and have overcome."

(Genesis 32:28)

More than once I have found myself in a tug of war in my prayer closet. In such times, there seemed to be a sense of urgency, a desperation, a calling to wrestle. I don't presume to fully grasp it for there is so much still unrevealed to us as we strive to live out the Kingdom in a fallen world.

In one of those times, I felt my spirit pushing me to cry out to God for a breakthrough, a touch from heaven. The premise I stood on was that we have a good Father who will not give us stone for bread (Mt 7:9-11). Even if I did not know for sure how my request would be granted, to the best of my understanding, what I was praying for seemed to be aligned with His character and His Word.

In this particular occasion, the intensity of compounded emotions came out in a loud plea. I had a longstanding wound whose effect I still felt, and I cried for a deeper healing. I longed to be changed!

I immediately thought about Jacob, the great patriarch of Israel. He experienced what I believe best exemplifies my own struggle. The remarkable episode in his life is found in Genesis 32. His whole life is told from Genesis 27 on, but I want to focus on the eve of his reunion with his estranged twin brother, Esau. Jacob is returning to his homeland after having fled two decades earlier and he is now terrified of facing Esau, from whom he had stolen the first-born blessing.

Those had been long years of hard work, deception, and toil. Jacob was tired of the physical and emotional distance of his exile and needed a touch from God to take away his fear, guilt, and shame. He no longer wanted to live in the shadow of the past, but desired to look to the future with hope and joy. He was desperate.

A wrestling match was the furthest thing from his mind. Genesis 32:24-29 narrates what took place then:

24 So Jacob was left alone, and a man wrestled with him till daybreak.
25 When the man saw that he could not overpower him, he touched the socket of Jacob's hip so that his hip was wrenched as he wrestled with the man.

26Then the man said, "Let me go, for it is daybreak." But Jacob replied, "I will not let you go unless you bless me."
27The man asked him, "What is your name?" "Jacob," he answered.
28Then the man said, "Your name will no longer be Jacob, but Israel, because you have struggled with God and with humans and have overcome."
29Jacob said, "Please tell me your name."
But he replied, "Why do you ask my name?" Then he blessed him there.
30So Jacob called the place Peniel, saying, "It is because I saw God face to face and yet my life was spared."

The text says the man provoked him to a fight. At some point during the fight, Jacob realized that this man was sent from the Lord and had the power to bless him. Oh, how he desperately needed that blessing!

Throughout his life, Jacob had adamantly pursued the blessings, but had relied on his own deceitful ways to get them. God wanted to change that, but first Jacob needed to admit his weakness and surrender. His wrestle was a physical demonstration of a deep yearning that resides in every human heart: a father's blessing. Years before he had tricked his father into blessing him, but it had not satisfied or changed him. He was now struggling with his old self. He had let go of his former identity to allowed himself to be transformed by God.

"I will not let you go unless you bless me!"

I had found myself in a similar situation. Patterns, habits, mindsets become rooted in us, but we must die to our fallen selves to make room for our new identity in Him. Like Jacob, I longed to be transformed and I was willing to wrestle with God for it.

At first, it may be a need, a troublesome situation or a wound that leads us to God. However, as we get closer to Him, we realize what we really need is God himself. When Jacob realized he was wrestling with a heavenly person, he knew he could be changed and he would not let this chance pass him by. The greater blessing Jacob found was being face to face with the Lord, who always responds when we seek Him in humility and desperation. I believe it would be safe to assume there were more words spoken than what the text reveals.

"Have you heard God's blessing in your inmost being? Are the words, "You are my beloved child, in whom I delight" an endless source of joy and strength? Have you sensed, through the Holy Spirit, God speaking to you? That blessing – the blessing through the Spirit that is ours through Christ – is what Jacob received. Only that blessing makes idols unnecessary. As with Jacob, we usually discover this only after a life of "looking for blessings in all the wrong places." It often takes an experience of crippling weakness for us to finally discover it. That is why so many of the most God-blessed people limp as they dance for joy." [4]

That night had started with Jacob scared out of his wits at the thought of re-encountering his brother, but ended with a changed man, confident in the face of what was before him.

As for me, change did not happen all in that one moment, rather, I was set on a course where I have gradually experienced new levels of healing and freedom. It was worth pleading with God.

REFLECTIONS

The manner in which God responded to the desire of Jacob's heart was unusual, but it shows it was aligned with His will.

- **Do you identify with Jacob in his struggle?**
- **In your life, what things have moved you towards God? What changes have come about as a result?**

CHAPTER 17
FAITH IN ACTION

And without faith it is impossible to please God, because anyone who comes to him must believe that he exists and that he rewards those who earnestly seek him.

(Hebrews 11:6)

How do you evaluate your level of faith? Our tendency is to think others have more than we do. If you consider your faith to be small, the good news is that it can grow. God alone knows our hearts, and He responds to even the tiniest seeds of faith in us.

Jesus affirmed faith wherever He found it. When a bleeding woman dared to touch Him, believing she would be healed, he said: *"Daughter, your faith has healed you. Go in peace and be freed from your suffering."* (Mark 5:34).

When a Roman centurion appealed to Jesus to heal one of his servants, the Lord was pleased with the faith and humility of this gentile leader. The centurion's message said: "I do not deserve to have you come under my roof. That is why I did not even consider myself worthy to come to you. But say the word, and my servant will be healed." This Roman officer recognized the authority Jesus had and asked him to exercise it. Jesus said to the crowd following him, *"I tell you, I have not found such great faith even in Israel."* Luke 7:6-9

Jesus was not shy about challenging his closest friends when they didn't exercise faith, like the time He and His disciples were on a boat amidst a violent storm. Jesus was asleep at the stern of the boat. Terrified, the disciples woke Jesus up and pleaded for him to save them. Jesus rebuked the storm but then He rebuked them. The disciples had seen many miracles, but they still reacted in fear. Jesus said to them, *"Why are you so afraid? Do you still have no faith?"* (Mark 4:39-40).

Given the reprimand the disciples received, do you doubt what would have happened if they had rebuked the storm themselves? Jesus always honors the faith we place in him. It is not a matter of being presumptuous, but of trust in God, in his Word and his character. Such faith leads to action.

In the same way, faith by itself, if it is not accompanied by action, is dead.

(James 2:17)

In His divine wisdom, God doesn't show the whole journey that awaits us on our path of faith. He invites to a step-by-step journey, growing stronger in faith as we experience more of His faithfulness along the way. Like exercising at the gym, we begin with light weights and as our muscles become stronger, we increase the weight. The faith "muscle" that you exercise today will be strong enough to bear the challenges that await in your tomorrow.

One thing to remember when taking small or large steps of faith – God is always good. He delights in answering prayers of faith that reflect His goodness. Like the time Beto and I heard about the upcoming wedding of a dear friend in the United States. She had been a missionary partner and a bridesmaid in our wedding, so attending her wedding was important to us. We also had a longing to return to the USA to reconnect with friends and churches there and to introduce our daughter who was 2 years old then. But we didn't have money for such a big trip.

On the day we received the wedding invitation, I said to Beto: "If Cirleia is getting married, I am going to her wedding!" He responded, "If you are going, then so am I!" We laughed in the face of the miracle it would be to receive what we needed to get there. Together we said a prayer that went something like this: "Father, we want to participate in this wedding, but for that to happen, we depend on a miracle of provision. If you desire to bless us with this trip, we ask that you provide for it, and we will give all the glory to you. Amen."

Having worked on the mission field for most of our married life, many times Beto and I had seen God provide miraculously, often at the eleventh hour. Because of the logistics of such a trip, we asked that He provide earlier this time if He wanted us to attend. The way in which God chose to respond certainly surprised us.

A few weeks later, we were serving as translators for a national worship gathering taking place near São Paulo. At this event, one of the keynote speakers approached Beto and said: "I overheard you talking about a trip you'd like to make to the US. Can you tell me more about it?" Surprised, Beto explained about the wedding and our tentative plans. The man replied: "I want to finance this trip. I have a special reserve, and I feel I need to bless your family with it. I will cover the airfare and the car rental." Beto thanked him, still in shock from the offer. A few minutes later, he burst into our room to give me the news. I started crying and shouting praise to God! We couldn't hide our joy.

We could have never imagined the incredible way the Lord would choose to respond to our prayer! God used someone Beto barely knew as an instrument to answer our prayer of faith.

Months later, we celebrated God's goodness again – at Larry and Cirleia's wedding. Whenever possible and appropriate, we share this testimony of God's gracious answer to our simple prayer of faith. Our greatest joy is to see the name of Jesus glorified through this!

REFLECTIONS

When we take first steps of faith, a creation movement is set into motion in the spirit world. As always, God is the initiator. He removes obstacles, heals bodies and minds, breaks bondages, and provides abundantly to achieve His purposes in us. In response to our faith, He gives us the privilege of participating in the creation.

Therefore I tell you, whatever you ask for in prayer, believe that you have received it, and it will be yours.
(Mark 11:24)

- **How have you been working out your faith "muscle"?**
- **What is the next step of faith God is asking you to take?**

CHAPTER 18

AN OVERFLOWING CUP

And when he had taken it, the four living creatures and the twenty-four elders fell down before the Lamb. Each one had a harp, and they were holding golden bowls full of incense, which are the prayers of God's people.
(Revelation 5:8)

When we begin to pray for something or someone, we embark on an adventure. It's like entering a forest without a map. We don't know where the path will take us, but our Heavenly Guide does. In the secret place, we take our requests to God without knowing how He will lead us. We simply trust in the Father's good heart.

In the dark forest we are sometimes tempted to give up. God asks us to persist until we get to where He wants us:

Ask and it will be given to you; seek and you will find; knock and the door will be opened to you. For everyone who asks receives; the one who seeks finds; and to the one who knocks, the door will be opened.

(Matthew 7:7-8)

How long should we persist in prayer for a certain request? I cannot give a specific answer, but you will recognize when the cup is full. There are requests on my prayer list that, happily, are checked off quickly. Others stay for a season and still others that have been there for over 20 years! It often seems like many of our requests are answered late. It is hard to wait for an answer, but we are being transformed as we pray, and so are the ones we pray for.

For those requests continuing for months or years, perseverance in faith is necessary to shake loose spiritual obstacles. Prophet Daniel's prayer for Israel demonstrated there is often an invisible battle raging that must be won before we receive the answer. Satan's forces tried to stop the answer to Daniel's prayer from arriving. But the Lord's angel prevailed and said:

"Do not be afraid, Daniel. Since the first day that you set your mind to gain understanding and to humble yourself before your God, your words were heard, and I have come in response to them. But the prince of the Persian kingdom resisted me twenty-one days. Then Michael, one of the chief princes, came to help me, because I was detained there with the king of Persia.

(Daniel 10:12-13)

I once heard Darlene Cunningham, co-founder of Youth With A Mission, say this: "There is a moment in which our spirit discerns when a specific prayer has been heard. We sense we no longer need to ask, but only wait for the answer to come to fruition." She identified this with the expression "prayed through." I understood what she meant as I have experienced it myself. In the secret place, you will come to recognize when the cup is full.

In Prayer that Works, a bestseller released in Brazil by Bethany Publishing House, we find this quote:

> "Praying men and women agonize before God in prayer for some blessing that they know to be in accordance with his will, because of the promises found in the pages of the Scriptures. They pray for hours and hours, or even for days, when, suddenly, the Holy Spirit reveals to them, in a clear and absolute way, that God has already given them what they asked for; they feel confident that they no longer need to send petitions to God about the issue. It is as if God had said, with all clarity: "Your prayer has been heard, and I have already answered your heart's desire." This is not just one man's experience, but of the many who make prayer the foundation of their lives, they will be able to bear witness to the same fact. It is also not a one-time experience in their lives. It occurs over and over again."

When Beto and I were engaged, one of the items of many on our list of preparations was our honeymoon. We planned the trip we wanted with much care and anticipation. Our travel agent put together a package that included a few days in Buenos Aires and a few extra ones in Patagonia – beautiful places for couples in love to visit.

We prayed for months for everything that was involved in our wedding. We didn't know how all the expenses would be paid but there was a strong conviction in my heart that God was pleased with our marriage and would provide for our plans. As the wedding date drew near, expenses of various kinds were covered, but not the honeymoon expenses. The travel agent graciously held the reservation, but with three weeks left until the big event, we still didn't have the money for the trip. Beto, attempting to lighten the blow of disappointment for me, said: "Love, I think it might be good for us to have a Plan B for our honeymoon that isn't as expensive."

With a confidence that surprised even me, I heard myself responding: "Honey, our honeymoon will be Plan A, I am sure of it, don't ask me how."

A few days before the wedding, we traveled to Belo Horizonte for a luncheon to celebrate with family and friends who would not be able to attend the religious ceremony in Curitiba. At the event, Beto sat next to a friend of his that I didn't know. With a big smile, he asked us: "What is still pending on your gifts list?"

Beto laughed and said:

"Oh various things, anything ranging from picture frames to our honeymoon!" "Do you know where you are going on your honeymoon?"

"Yes," Beto said, "We have reservations made for an entire package."

"Well, as you already have it planned out, you can check it off your list, it will be my present to you."

I almost fell off my chair when I heard it. The first chance I got, I took Beto aside and holding his arm, I asked: "Love, I hope he is not playing with a bride's dream, is this for real?" It was true. He paid for our entire honeymoon – Plan A!

That day as we left the celebration, we weren't walking, we were floating!

The only thing I had done was trust in the still small voice in my heart that whispered a promise: "I am happy with your wedding and want to give you what you are dreaming about." God is faithful to His promises. The only appropriate response was our thankfulness.

REFLECTIONS

On our journey with Christ, we build a story of friendship and partnership, that is marked by prayer.

- **Have you documented answers to prayer in your life?**
- **Have you ever experienced a full cup in this way? How did it go?**

CHAPTER 19
MEMORIALS

Praise the Lord, my soul, and forget not all his benefits.
(Psalm 103:2)

We are prone to forgetfulness, and sometimes that's a good thing. Just as the Lord forgives and forgets our sins (Isaiah 43:25), we also should be quick to forgive and forget offenses against us. But, if we are not intentional, we may forget that which we absolutely should not. God well knows this human tendency and, for that reason, instructed His people to build monuments.

The term itself is self-explanatory: a memorial is something we build to remind us of some event or person. It is the documentation of an important occurrence. To followers of Christ, it is a way keep alive the memories of blessings we have received and maintain a thankful heart.

Let this be written for a future generation, that a people not yet created may praise the Lord: (Psalm 102:18).

In the fourth chapter of Joshua, we find the Lord's instructions about stones that were to be picked up from the Jordan River to create a monument for future generations.

"And said to them: 'Go over before the ark of the Lord your God into the middle of the Jordan. Each of you is to take up a stone on his shoulder, according to the number of the tribes of the Israelites, to serve as a sign among you. In the future, when your children ask you, 'What do these stones mean?' tell them that the flow of the Jordan was cut off before the ark of the covenant of the Lord. When it crossed the Jordan, the waters of the Jordan were cut off. These stones are to be a memorial to the people of Israel forever."

(Joshua 4:5-7)

This was just one occasion, but throughout the Bible we find various examples of monuments. The Israelites were known as a people of rituals and feasts and we also need to constantly be reminded of who God is, His miracles, and His faithfulness for there will always be new challenges. These truths must be well established in our minds. Furthermore, the duty is ours to tell the stories of His deeds for generations to come.

Let this be written for a future generation, that a people not yet created may praise the Lord: (Psalm 102:18)

Memorials come in different forms as Beto and I discovered when visiting friends in another city. Leaning against one of the living room walls there was a small shelf with keepsakes on careful display. Intrigued, we inquired what they meant. There was a pair of baby shoes and other objects we couldn't quite identify. The couple's three children were adults and for that reason, we found the baby shoes a bit odd.

As soon as we asked, a smile spread across their faces. "We placed them as a visual reminder to help us pray for our children frequently and intensely," they said.

Their children were young adults but were in a season in which they were making important decisions in their lives. Each time the parents passed through the living room and saw the objects on that shelf, it helped to fan the flame of perseverance in prayer for their children. We knew this couple well, and their little memorial reflected their intimacy in the secret place. At the time, our daughter was very young, but that demonstration blessed and inspired us for years to come.

We are sensory beings, with sight being one of the most important senses. Having something concrete and visual in front of us is a powerful tool to preserve that which we shouldn't allow ourselves to forget.

I have several notebooks stored away that have decades of written prayers. I write what I don't want to risk forgetting. When I leave this world, my journals will remain as a written testimony of God's grace and faithfulness to future generations. Who knows, perhaps even more people might be blessed by this?

Another habit we have adopted in our home is a "Thankfulness Jar." We keep ours in the living room. The idea is that weekly, each one writes on small pieces of paper at least one thing they are thankful for. The jar fills up, and at the end of the year we open and re-read the notes to be reminded of how good and faithful God is.

REFLECTIONS

Monuments are reminders of people and situations that will be a testimony of the faithfulness and power of God in your life. Think about what they were in your life.

- **What are the lessons and the values they contain?**
- **How can you maintain and pass on these memories through the years?**

CHAPTER 20
HARVEST

Let us not become weary in doing good, for at the proper time we will reap a harvest if we do not give up.

(Galatians 6:9)

The walls of my secret place have witnessed tears and battles; much more than I would have liked. It is the nature of planting. Perhaps your seeding has also been with pain and obstacles. Tears are a part of the package we call life, and no one escapes them. What makes the difference is where we spill them. When we do this at Jesus' feet, in the secret place, we have the Father's company. He understands our pain and comforts us.

Even as I write, my eyes water with tears as I remember some precious seeds I have sown that are still under the ground. I can't see what is happening neither can I know how long it will take. At the right time, these seedlings will break through the surface.

Those who go out weeping, carrying seed to sow, will return with songs of joy, carrying sheaves with them.
(Psalm 126:6)

It's a constant challenge to maintain focus on eternal things because everything around us encourages us to look to the here and now. Voices seduce and incite us to spend time, energy, and resources on that which will remain here. Jesus instructs us to store our treasures in heaven and plant seeds that will bear fruit in eternity.

But store up for yourselves treasures in heaven, where moths and vermin do not destroy, and where thieves do not break in and steal.
(Matthew 6:20)

Often, we sow in sacrifice and may not be the ones to reap the fruit of the seeds planted. There is comfort in knowing our work is not in vain; our sacrifices are small when compared to the blessing of bringing someone into joy that has no end in our true home.

Even now the one who reaps draws a wage and harvests a crop for eternal life, so that the sower and the reaper may be glad together.
(John 4:36)

I know that much of the good fruit I have reaped, and still do, is the result of the seeds my parents sowed with many tears. They have already passed, but I still receive the impact of their faithfulness. And just as I reap what others have sown, so others will reap what I have sown.

I sent you to reap what you have not worked for. Others have done the hard work, and you have reaped the benefits of their labor."

(John 4:38)

The Best Portion

God has given us the privilege of helping in His great harvest. Even if there was nothing to be harvested, we would have reason to be thankful and continue to faithfully serve Him. Just like David wrote long ago, what inheritance could be more beautiful than the Lord Himself ?

Lord, you alone are my portion and my cup; you make my lot secure. The boundary lines have fallen for me in pleasant places; surely I have a delightful inheritance.

(Psalm 16:5-6)

REFLECTIONS

As you ponder about the seeds you have sown, ask the Lord of the Harvest to search your heart and show you what He desires you to see.

- **Contemplate the seeds that you have planted. Will they bring the fruit you desire to harvest?**
- **What good fruits you reaped that others have planted?**

May we plant seeds of justice and faith that bring a harvest of joy to our hearts and glory to God!

NOTES:

Chapter 5: Above Fear

1. John and Statsi Eldredge, Captivating, unveiling the mistery of the feminine soul (USA, 2005), 115.

Chapter 6: Sufficient

2. Dr. Dan B. Allender, The Healing Path (USA, 2016), 189.

Chapter 13: Expectations

3. Antoine de Saint-Exupèry, The Little Prince (1943).

Chapter 16: Wrestling with God

4. Timothy Keller, Counterfeit Gods: The Empty Promises of Money, Sex, and Power, and the Only Hope that Matters, (USA, 2009).

Instagram: @raqueltavares7244
Facebook: Raquel Tavares
Email: raquel@viladolouvor.org
Website: raqueltavares.com.br/en

Raquel Tavares was born and raised in Curitiba, Southern Brazil. From childhood she has been voracious her reading and was deeply impacted by the in messages she was exposed to. Through this, her aptitude for writing and speaking was awakened.

Besides working as a translator and interpreter, she has also served as a missionary in Youth With Mission (YWAM) for over two decades within and outside Brazil.

She is married to Beto Tavares and they are parents to Nicole. They live in Cascais, Portugal and serve at Riverside Cascais International Church.

Share your reading experiences by writing to:
contato@autordafe.com.br

www.autordafe.com.br

AUTOR
DA FÉ

Printed in Great Britain
by Amazon

37665035R00078